The Photographs of William Rayson Smith

Volume I

The Photographs of William Rayson Smith

Volume I:
Norfolk and Beyond

Jennifer and David Boxall

Copyright © Jennifer and David Boxall.

This edition 2020 published by Poppyland Publishing, Lowestoft, NR32 3BB.

www.poppyland.co.uk

ISBN 978 1 909796 74 4

All rights reserved. No part of this publication may be reproduced, stored in a retrieval system or transmitted by any means, mechanical, photocopying, recording or otherwise, without the written permission of the publishers.

Designed and typeset in 10.5 on 13.5 pt Times New Roman.

Printed by Ashford Colour Press.

All images are from the authors' collection except p.80, which is in the collection of Matt Rix.

Royalties from this book have been kindly donated by the authors to the Royal National Institute for the Blind.

Contents

Preface	7
Introduction	9
Dickleburgh	11
Canada	24
Harleston	30
Family Visits	42
Odds And Ends	50
Norwich, Needham and Forncett	56
Churches	60
Lowestoft and Lingwood	62
William as Photographer	65
Billingford	72
Picnics and Celebrations	74
An Intimate Conclusion	78
Epilogue	80
Character List	81
Bibliography and Acknowledgements	82
Index	83

Sketch maps showing the position of places relevant to the book (not to scale).

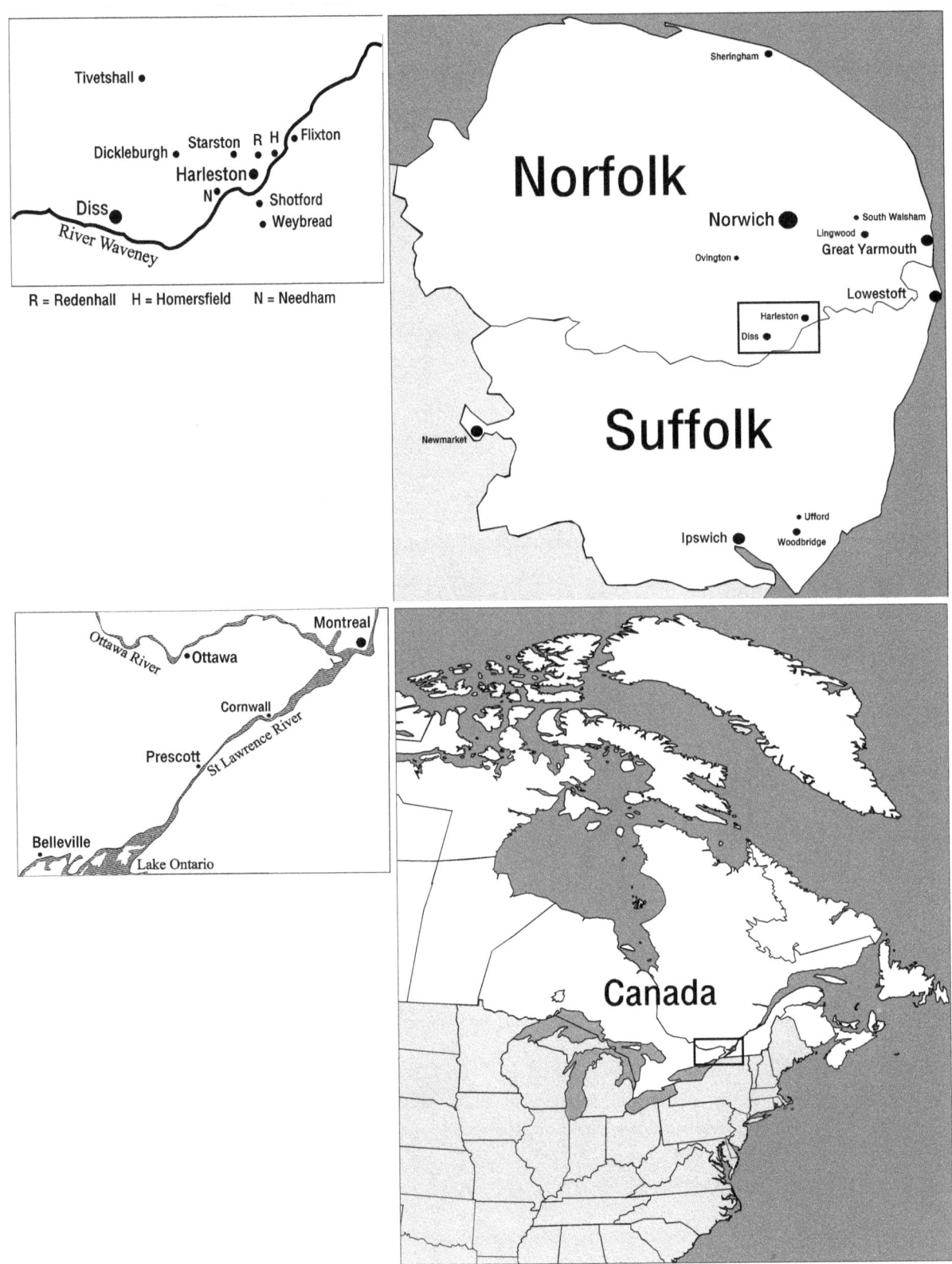

PREFACE

THE Lowestoft Journal of 24th May 1890 reports that when visiting Lowestoft the Prime Minister, Mr. Gladstone, was presented with "a valuable album with 50 splendid photographic views of the principal objects of interest in the neighbourhood." On receiving the gift he is reported to have said:

> I have already had the opportunity of turning over the leaves of this very beautiful album, and of looking at the admirable photographs it contains. I can assure you that the lovely scenes herein depicted are so well impressed upon my mind that I could have done without any photographs at all. But they are interesting in themselves; and will always be associated in my mind with pleasant memories.

We were fortunate to have "the greatest pleasure", as did Mr. Gladstone, when opening two late Victorian photograph albums found in the home of my aunt, in Lowestoft, following her death in 2011. In the albums were found "lovely scenes" of a multitude of different places and people, mainly in South Norfolk and Suffolk.

Many pictures beautifully illustrate Victorian social history. There are fascinating family groups of interest not only for our family history but also offering a taste of Victorian family life. Some scenes are clearly historically significant, such as photographs of alterations at Harleston Railway Station. Events are also recorded, such as parties for Queen Victoria's Golden Jubilee in Harleston and Dickleburgh. Some are surprising pictures, such as people dressed up for a Winter Carnival on The Waveney in 1895 and elephants in the street in Harleston. The photographs posed many questions. What was Hospital Sunday? Why photographs of Belleville in Canada? Many more will be posed by the photographs, some partly answered in the book and others still a mystery.

The question of who made the albums was quickly answered by the beautifully written signature in one of the albums—W.R. Smith. I was able to identify him from family history research as my mother's great uncle, the brother of her grandmother, Mary Rix, who lived in Lowestoft towards the end of her life. We assume that William had given the albums into her care, maybe because of the photographs of her family in the books. The albums stayed in the family in my aunt's care. Then the challenge was to find out about this talented early amateur photographer, his life and his photographs. This we have tried to do in the following pages.

Jen Boxall, 2020

INTRODUCTION

The Photographer

WILLIAM Rayson Smith was baptised in Dickleburgh Church on 10th October 1841. He died only five miles away in Harleston on 12th October 1932 and was buried in Dickleburgh Churchyard. His father also William (1812-1897) was the owner of the corn mill in Dickleburgh. William was his second child. In all he had five brothers and seven sisters. William, his father, was married three times, the first wife Mary, being William's mother. Rayson was her surname. The second wife, Anna was her sister.

The corn mill at Dickleburgh was a substantial business. It and the family home next to it appear in the photographs. It stood opposite the parish church. We can see that William grew up in comfortable surroundings. His education seems to have been at home because the 1852 census records six of the children as "scholar at home" and a governess. Possibly he went away to school in his teens.

In 1868 he married Maria Hudson at Redenhall Church. She was the daughter of Henry Lombard Hudson, of Harleston, who was another mill owner. The first photographs in the albums are of the mill house, still in existence today. Two of Maria's brothers, Ernest and Henry, appear later in the story.

Soon after their marriage William and Maria went to live in Belleville, Canada. They are recorded in Canada in the 1871 and 1881 censuses. They returned before 1887 as a photograph from 1887 in England appears in the albums. William appears to have taken up photography whilst in Canada. Thirty photographs of Belleville are included in the album.

The Smiths brought with them from Canada a girl born in 1874, Winifred Annie Colman. We have a census record of her parents and three siblings in Canada. Soon after Winifred arrived in England she went to Bedford to school as a boarder. In the 1911 census Winifred is described as William and Maria's adopted daughter. There are over twenty photographs of her in the albums and at least two probably taken by her which include William. She lived until 1962, remaining single.

William, Maria and Winifred lived in the Mill House at Harleston on their return from Canada until 1903 when Maria's brother Henry sold up house and mill to marry the widow of the proprietor of the Magpie inn in Harleston. They lived at the Magpie for a while and then at a house called Elmhurst in Harleston. Maria died in 1924.

Photographs opposite

Top left: William Rayson Smith and Maria standing with Samuel Smith playing chess probably with his elder sister Anna.

Top right: William Rayson's father, William, with his third wife Sarah.

Below: Maria Smith seated in the conservatory at Dickleburgh.

The Photographs

There are two albums: the first is of horizontal format, the second vertical. Each album weighs over five pounds and contains forty pages of thick, light brown card. The cardboard covers are finished and bound with leather and gold-coloured decoration. The older album has been professionally rebound. There are 328 photographs, and the dates in the albums show them to have been taken between the mid-1880s and 1899. All are half-plate in size, 6 x 4¼ inches with some cut down in size before mounting. William must have used a plate camera as roll-film was not available at the start of this period. Photographic enlargers were in the future so the photographs are contact prints, that is exactly the size of the glass plate. It would have been quite possible for William to have processed and printed the photographs himself or he could have used a professional. This would probably have been a chemist and several were in business in Harleston at the time. The prints are well done but the quality of some photographs is not very good. Many now show browning at the edges and some spotting, but on the whole, they are in very good condition.

The start date is significant for it is less than a decade after a major breakthrough in the chemistry of photographic materials, which had the practical effect of speeding up the taking of a photograph. It actually came to mean that a hand-held camera was possible, though a tripod was probably preferable. The sharpness of many of the photographs suggest use of a tripod; in fact, the detail on some is exceptional as revealed under a good magnifying glass.

We have chosen about 130 photographs for this book; about another 50 will appear in a subsequent book about Lowestoft. Of the remainder most are omitted because of duplication of subject matter or poor quality. We have done a minimum of digital manipulation where helpful to present a picture as clearly as possible. With some we have cropped the edges or an area poor on the original. We have also included some of William's captions in his own writing. Captions in italic are William's own words. We want William to speak to us as clearly as possible of all that he shows us of late Victorian life in South Norfolk.

DICKLEBURGH

WILLIAM mounted twenty-two photographs of Dickleburgh in his first album with photographs of Canada preceding them. We have moved these pictures to the beginning of this book as it was in Dickleburgh that William grew up and where his father and then his brother Sam lived, until 1917, in the family home at the Mill. He appears to have taken his new camera to Dickleburgh soon after his return from Canada. We can therefore date them at around 1887. He was living about five miles away in Harleston and it is interesting to ask how he travelled between the two places. He could easily have walked; we know he used a cycle and a pony and trap would also have been possible.

Dickleburgh is today a small, quiet Norfolk village. There is a mini supermarket. The Crown Hotel is still going strong, as is the Church. In William's day there was a second inn, The King's Head, and several businesses in The Street. Modern house names indicate, for example, a bakery and a forge, but the photographs show more. Dickleburgh was in a small way quite an important place even without the Smith's Mill. The village lies on the main road from Norwich to Ipswich which, until about thirty years ago when the bypass was built, ran through the narrow main street. Photographs exist of the traffic congestion people endured. However, the road brought business and was an important link to the outside world for hundreds of years. It is in fact a Roman Road, Pye Street, linking Caistor St. Edmund, near Norwich, to Colchester.

Many of the photographs show buildings much as they are today. Others, notably those of the Mill, are a historical record of what they were like and now gone for ever. Also, we have here the first of William's family portraits: his subjects look at the camera and are nicely posed. Their clothes and surroundings tell us much about the life and circumstances of a prosperous late Victorian family.

The village is on a small ridge running east to west, so that the main road rises gently to the top of the hill on which stands the church. Next to the church is the former King's Head inn and opposite it was the Smith's corn mill. The mill was on the corner of Rectory Road, formerly White Horse Road, leading to the village of Rushall. Lee Cottage orphanage, now a private house, is in this road, as was a windmill that was in business throughout the nineteenth century. At the bottom of The Street is a crossroads, the main arm of which was a road westward towards Shimpling and Burston. Burston had a station on the Norwich to London rail line. Smith's Mill had siding facilities at this station, about three miles from the mill. This station was also, of course, a link for the village to the wider world. The Smiths may well have used it to reach their business premises on Castle Hill in Norwich.

Dickleburgh St. North.

Dickleburgh St. South.

The Crown Inn.

Houses further up with roadworks.

Corner House, Dickleburgh.

The Smith's mill and house were to the left and behind. The churchyard trees are to the right with the King's Head sign top right.

Dickleburgh Church

A scene no longer possible today. The church is obscured by trees. The Smith's house behind the church is gone, as are the other houses and the mill buildings, replaced by twentieth century houses. The Smith's graves are under the large tree.

Dickleburgh garden

We see a view from the other direction. The house is large, although possibly didn't feel so when there were nine children and their governess to fit in. The two men are probably the gardener and one of the Smiths.

Mill Yard Dickleburgh.

Mill Yard Dickleburgh.

These are the only original prints of William's found by us to have been published elsewhere. They show the site in about 1887. The top photograph shows the mill house; the garden and the greenhouses are behind the building on the left - home and work on one site.

The bottom photograph faces the other way. Was the yard always so clean and tidy? As with many of the photographs use of a magnifying glass brings up detail.

Lee Cottage

Lee Cottage was opened in 1883 by the Rev. Henry Brandreth, Rector of Dickleburgh, and his wife Louisa. Lee Cottage was the second home for orphaned girls in Dickleburgh. Rose Cottage, the first, was certified on 27 June 1880 to receive destitute girls placed by the Board of Guardians, created by the local Poor Law Union, who administered poor relief and the workhouse system. Rose Cottage can still be seen opposite the Old Reading Room. The girls were sent to the local school and, as it was expected that they would go into domestic service, they were also trained in essential domestic skills, including needlework.

The Rev. Brandreth and Louisa took a great interest in the care of the girls as did some other local residents. A Miss Mayo gave £300 for the renovation and upkeep of Lee House. The Rev. Brandreth set aside a patch in the churchyard, that can still be seen today, for the burial of girls from the homes. Eight girls are believed to be buried there.

In July 1888 the homes were taken over by the Waifs and Strays Society with Mrs. Brandreth becoming the Honorary Local Secretary for the Society. Lee Cottage was closed in 1895 but Rose Cottage continued, as did a local fostering scheme in which Mrs. Brandreth was involved.

"Lee Cottage" Orphan Home Dickleburgh.

Dickleburgh Millhouse Garden

The main feature of the garden was the pond. We can see water lilies and irises. It was known to be supplied with warm water from the mill leading to very large goldfish! There were also two circular fountains near the house. A large greenhouse backed onto the mill buildings and was probably heated from it. Behind the figures in the top picture was a tennis court and orchard. The figures here are probably Sam Smith, William's wife, Maria and one of William's sisters. The dog is unnamed.

Here we see the fountains and the house. In the background we see the conservatory where the photograph of Maria Smith was taken (see p.8).

Dickleburgh Hall

The hall still exists and a recent owner added a golf course. It was built in the 16th century and owned by a Mr. Glebe in the 1700s. He saw, then, that the Suffolk Punch horse was under threat and decided to improve the breed. All current bloodstock goes back to his efforts. In the early 21st century the breed is again under threat with barely enough animals existing for its survival. This is the first of a number of William's photographs of "Halls."

Dickleburgh Moor 1887

The moor was an area of peaty wetland near Dickleburgh Hall. It regularly froze in winter so skating was a popular winter outing.

A tea party in the garden of Dickleburgh Mill House. We cannot tell the occasion, perhaps Winifred's birthday as she features in both pictures in a distinctive hat. The woman in black is William's wife, Maria.

The graves are of William's brother and sister who both died young. The row of graves was extended towards us and eventually included the grave of William and Maria.

Simply captioned "Tivetshall" by William. We do not know why this house and its occupants were important to him. It is another of the local houses he photographed.

The Rectory of William's time was replaced soon after.

Interior Dickleburgh Church.

Dickleburgh garden, winter

Jubilee Dinner, Dickleburgh 1887

It looks as if everyone in the village is here. This one really does repay close examination with a magnifying glass.

DICKLEBURGH PARISH MAGAZINE, JUNE. 188

Although we ought at all times and in all places to look up in gratitude for the blessings of daily life, and above all for our constant strengthening and refreshing in body, soul, and spirit, yet still it is well that we should at special times realize how much we owe; and weekly Sabbaths by God's appointment, and birthdays, and the close of the year by the common consent of mankind, have been profitably used to bring to mind our long-continued blessings. God gave the Jews many rules which are no longer binding on us, but which are full of wisdom, and exactly fitted to the nature of man, for they were planned and arranged by God, who created man, and knows what is in him. One of their institutions was that at the end of every fifty years they had a jubilee year of special rejoicing. Men who had been obliged by poverty to part with their land had it restored to them. All who were slaves to their brethren were set free, and even labour on the fields was stopped. God provided for them when they rested and rejoiced in what He had done. And this was called the year of Jubilee. Hence it has been common when anything has gone on for fifty years to keep a Jubilee, to show in some marked way that we thank God who has brought us so far.

And we are called during this month to celebrate the remarkable fact of our good Queen having reigned for fifty years among us.

It is a plain fact, well-known to everybody, that these fifty years have been a time of unexampled peace and prosperity; that the state of the nation is improved beyond what anybody could have dared to hope. The Queen has been the chief ruler for fifty years, and she has made no mistakes, all she has undertaken has turned out well; and every Englishman and Englishwoman thinks of every act of her life, private or public, with pride and pleasure.

The Queen will be the first to give all glory to God for every good thing that has come to pass. Nobody has any reason to be told that the best of her unaided thoughts and efforts would have done very little.

But we know, on the other hand, how much mischief, public and private, would have followed if she had done wrong, politically, socially, or morally, and we do, therefore, feel great gratitude for all that has turned out so well. We read of many kings and queens whose lives have corrupted the morals, and whose folly has ruined the prosperity of their countries; and whilst we join with the Queen in giving thanks for the blessings and prosperity of the reign to God, who orders and disposes all things, our human hearts and affections also turn with the warmest gratitude and good feeling to the noble lady who has been permitted so many years of usefulness and good example among us.

Every child may read with pleasure of her simple, diligent, religious childhood. Every woman will feel pride in the useful life of the wife and mother. Every man admires the sterling good sense and honest purpose of all that she says and does. Every Christian is thankful that amidst the splendour and distraction of the Court of the richest country in the world, the Queen has never put her religion in the second place, but has been foremost in sympathy for all the afflictions of the poorest of her people, and kept herself unspotted from the world.

We are all called to promote by every means in our power the gladness of national thanksgiving; and I can think of no simpler and better rule than to treat the Queen and her day as you know she would treat you if for fifty years you had been a tried and valued servant to her as she has most certainly been the most valuable public servant of the nation. Her Majesty has not lived away from her people; her life as woman, wife, and mother has been more fully before the country than your own life has been known to your next-door neighbour, and we know and admire her kind heart and gentle character. And so I say to each, think how she would be thoughtful and wise to make glad the heart of her servant of fifty years; and do you, in your station, show a Queen-like care for others, a hearty sympathy to do the right and kind thing; do you make glad the heart of the least of her subjects; first giving all praise and glory to God, and then receiving or distributing His good gifts with cheerfulness.

Your servant for Jesus' sake, HENRY BRANDRETH.

The Rector's view on the Jubilee celebrations reflected the goodwill felt towards the Queen in 1887.

CANADA

WILLIAM and Maria went to Canada in 1870. On the 1881 Canadian census William is described as a "clerk"—a very general term for an office-worker. First thoughts are that he worked as an agent for his father's or father-in-law's corn business but we have no evidence for this. Certainly, many people emigrated to Canada at this time. It was an exciting time to be there. Belleville, where they settled, shared in an enormous growth of trade being in the County of Hastings, West Canada, where there had been a gold rush a few years before. This was reported in British newspapers including the Norwich Mercury of 5th January 1867 and could have alerted William to the attractions of the area.

Belleville then had a population of about 6000 and was growing. The town is at the mouth of the Moira River on the bay of Quinte on the north side of Lake Ontario. William and Maria would have sailed into the St. Lawrence River and then travelled the remaining three hundred miles or so by river boat or taken the still growing Grand Trunk Railway. This opened in 1852 and formed, and still forms, the main rail route across Canada from east to west.

William took up photography during his time in Belleville and mounted about thirty photographs in his first album. Many show scenes of rather empty new streets and buildings, including his house. A major industry was timber. William gives us two forest scenes and two of timber on the river. There is another picture in which he has cut off top and bottom of two photographs and joined them edgeways to show a panorama of the river bank. In front is an enormous stretch of logs in the water, but perhaps the background is more interesting. It shows the buildings of Belleville including church spires and industrial buildings. The first Canadian photograph is of Belleville Post Office, grandiose and probably new. It carries a sign RAILWAY CROSSING, either meaning a tram or train. The lines are just visible. There is also a poster advertising "Fedora" at the Opera House.

The Smiths left Canada in 1886 or 1887. The last years there were not without sadness. Two of Maria's brothers had joined them, but died in 1881 and 1885. And Maria's father had died in Harleston in 1885, suggesting a possible motive for their return to England was to be with her mother and perhaps for William to help in the corn-mill business with her brother Henry.

"W.R. Smith. Belleville". We do not know if the Smiths owned or rented the white house. We get a good idea of the growing town with its rather English looking houses, a board walk for pavement and what may be either a factory or tenements in the background. A fact we do know about William's time in Belleville is that he was, for a time, the neighbour of a Dr. McCoun and helped him with his collection of mosses.

W. R. Smith, Belleville

Post Office Belleville, Canada.

Rafting square timber, Belleville.

Timber coming down river, Belleville

A Clearing in the Woods, Canada.

A Canadian Elm, Canada.
(see manal. foot of tree)

Suspension Bridge, Belleville.

'St. Thomas' Church Belleville

Canadian Passenger Boat

The 377 ton Bohemian paddle steamer was built in the early 1870s. Part of the Cornwall Line it carried passengers between Montreal, Cornwall and Prescott along the St Lawrence river. It was the last 'side-wheeler' to run the St. Lawrence rapids with passengers and may have been the Smiths' transport to Montreal on their return journey.

Parisian 5600 Tons

The Parisian was the finest of Allen Line's trans-atlantic ships built by Robert Napier & Sons, Glasgow, in 1881. She could easily accommodate 120 second-class and 1,000 steerage passengers and is possibily the ship taken by the Smiths on their return to Britain.

HARLESTON

THE Smiths had returned to England to live in the Mill House in Harleston by the summer of 1887. Harleston, a small market town, is Maria's birthplace and about five miles east of Dickleburgh. Maria was the daughter of an important local businessman, Henry Lombard Hudson, originally from Wisbech in Cambridgeshire. He had died in 1885 leaving the business to his son Henry, who lived in the Mill House with his mother, Caroline. The Smiths came to live with them and were here throughout the period of the albums. The house still exists and for many years was home to the Millhouse Pottery. The ivy, the big gates and the projection over the doorway have gone but much is the same. Many of William's photographs of people were taken in the yard behind the house set against doorways and a pump that are still there. The photograph "Cleaning Time" is one of these. The current owner was kind enough to show us inside. What looks like a building of one period is not so; to the left on the photo the upstairs room is half-timbered, suggesting its origins several hundred years ago. The age of the front is probably that of a brick inscribed "HLH 1868" recorded in a late 19th century directory. The owner did not know of the brick, but one is missing from the wall next to the gate post. Presumably an earlier owner took it as a souvenir! HLH stands for Henry Lombard Hudson so we assume that he had the front built on in 1868. It is also the possible year of his acquisition of the mill.

Winifred Annie Colman, whom the Smiths brought with them from Canada, stands in the doorway in "Cleaning Time", aged about 13. This is the first of over twenty photographs William took of her. Usually, as here, she looks boldly at the camera. There are a couple of pictures of William, probably taken by her, including him on the tricycle. So, we can follow Winifred, in the photographs, as she grows to be a young woman. Her parents were from Norfolk and are recorded, with four children, living in a town near Belleville, Canada, in 1881. The Smiths regarded her as a daughter and she was described in the 1911 census as "adopted daughter". She lived with them, apart from when she was away at school in Bedford. She died in Harleston in 1962 at the age of 88, unmarried and had inherited William's money. We have, in fact, already met her on "Dickleburgh Moor. 1887", central and looking right at us as usual.

William lived in Harleston for 45 years. His photographic activities in the first dozen years were twofold. He took local scenes and he took pictures of family. We have arranged his photographs as near as possible in the order in which he mounted them, which seems likely to be more or less the order in which he took them. However, some we have moved to fit with a theme or subject.

Above: The Mill House.

Right: Cleaning Time with Winifred Annie Colman in the doorway.

Two popular walks, from which William mounted photographs throughout his albums, were to the River Waveney at Shotford Bridge on the south side of Harleston and to the River Beck about a mile north of his home. The church is at Starston, taken across the tributary bridge, a scene not possible today because there are many more trees.

From Starston Bridge

This looks east along the Beck. The meadow to the right is now a locally run open space.

Starston Meadows.

Shotford Bridge

Mills

The Harleston windmill (left) had belonged to Henry Lombard Hudson. It was sold in 1885, after his death, to his son Henry, but probably occupied by another son, Thompson. It was taken down in 1916 but the house survives. Most windmills in the east of England are, as shown on the left, brick-built tower mills. Post-mills are the other type, an example of which was recorded by William for posterity at Weybread (right). Its base is of brick but not tapered as in a tower mill. This was a magnificent example, standing in the open fields some way from the village. It has not survived.

Weybread water mill was nearer the village, which is on the south side of the River Waveney and so in Suffolk. It burnt down on February 6th 1920 so again this photograph is a valuable record for posterity. It was a magnificent building of three stories, the lower being of brick. At some point an engine was installed for use when the river's flow did not provide enough power. William mounted four photographs of it. We have here the two best.

Note: much information on all the mills William photographed can be found on the Norfolk Mills Society website.

Weybread Water Mill.

The Railway

William lived a couple of hundred yards from Harleston Station. All the photographs we have away from Harleston from now on in the albums suggest that he travelled by train. He visited his three married sisters and his father's retirement home in Lowestoft. He went to Bedford where Winifred was at school. He travelled to Newmarket and as far as Dorking in Surrey for reasons we do not know. Other photographs are of Norwich near to the site of the Smith's business premises and of Sheringham, probably as a tourist.

The importance of the railway was great for him and for Harleston people. There are seven railway photographs, all important historical documents, four from about 1887 and three from 1894. Indeed, we have found no earlier than that on a 1904 postcard. For this and much information we acknowledge our use of *Tivetshall to Beccles. The Waveney Line.* (See bibliography.)

Harleston Station opened on 2nd November 1860 and closed to passengers on 5th January 1953. Daily trains to Norwich, taking about 35 minutes, and also to Beccles, gave excellent connections to all the places he photographed.

The railway was very important for freight. Every station in the country was served by pick-up goods trains which, before motor transport, brought in everything needed by shops and other businesses. The ubiquitous import was coal. Local products, mostly agricultural, were sent out. The two local mills used the railway and had their own sidings.

An interesting feature of this photo is the signal at top left. It is an early 'somersault' type. This probably was replaced in the alterations noted on page 69 to the type with which we are more familiar today.

Harleston Station

A Norwich bound train but no obvious passengers wait. This is the only part of the station to survive to this day. Spotty photograph!

Railway Bridge. Harleston

This crossed Redenhall Road immediately to the east of the station and is no longer in existence. It is a very clear photograph, except for the train which the slow camera shutter speed could not freeze. The locomotive is a very elegant GER 2-4-0 tender engine, the coaches six wheelers. Notice the road surface and the distant horse drawn vehicle. The young girl is placed to give a well composed photograph.

Harleston Bridge

Not quite such a good composition but it includes the coal merchant premises. This building still stands as a private house. The business had its own private siding and a small triangular yard with a large shed just visible to the left of the building.

Harleston - Queen's Jubilee

The weekly *Ipswich Journal* of Friday June 3rd 1887 reported that a meeting of the General Committee was held in the Reading Room. The Archdeacon Perowne presided and there was a good attendance.

The report goes on to say, "It was intimated that provision would have to be made for 1,200 adults and 600 children. The contract for supplies of meat by Messrs. Beare, Charlish and Miles was accepted, and a contract was also entered in with Messrs. Smith, Murkett, and Edwards, bakers, for the supply of bread and for necessary baking. The Committee also accepted Messrs. B. and A. Rayner's offer to provide the necessary tables and table cloths for the sum of £14 10s.

"The question of the allowance of beer at dinner and afterwards was productive of a lively discussion. It was ultimately decided to allow it.

"The Committee voted the sum of £23 for carrying out the sports programme, and the sum of £15, and if possible, £20, for the display of fireworks.

"A suggestion was made that Jubilee medals be provided for the children, and this matter, together with the appointment of a ladies' committee, to carry out the children's tea and sports, will be duly considered."

Starston Jubilee Sports.

1887 Jubilee Dinner, Harleston, Suk.

Redenhall and Harleston are one ancient parish although both are mentioned in the Doomsday survey. Both photographs show the main road from Thetford and Diss to Beccles and Lowestoft. Both places are now bypassed. These views are very recognisable today. Redenhall has a very fine medieval church; Harleston, the much bigger place, only had a chapel of ease until a parish church was built in 1872. Harleston Market is ancient, first mentioned in 1369 and still functioning.

Left: *Redenhall Church*
Below: *Thoroughfare*
Harleston's main street taken from the Market Place.

Two photographs in the yard of the Mill House. The people include family members and servants. Work has been interrupted for the photographer. Both photographs feature empty boots and the hedge separating the yard from the garden, used for drying buckets.

FAMILY VISITS

WILLIAM returned from Canada to find three of his sisters married, with children, and living some way from Harleston. The train provided an easy way to get to see them.

Family Visit 1: South Walsham

Mary Smith married Spencer Rix in 1877. Their daughter Ethnie Eva was Jen's grandmother, born in 1886, and is probably the little girl on the donkey. We will meet the twins in the pushchair again as teenagers. Oddly two older brothers are not here, perhaps at school.

The photograph is actually at South Walsham, reached by train via Norwich to Lingwood Station. Spencer Rix farmed 30 acres but is described in the 1881 census as a merchant and miller employing 12 men, 2 clerks and a boy and, as we can see here, a nanny. He came from Thrandeston near Diss where his ancestors had owned Goswold Hall. The family has a memorial and grave spaces in Thrandeston churchyard. There is a second photograph of this family about 10 years later. William took photographs in the surrounding area which give us an impression of the Norfolk Broads at that time. The captions are his.

N. Walsham.

Staithe, South Walsham

South Walsham Broad

On the Bure

Family Visit 2: Woodbridge

William's youngest sister Joanna married Edward Eaton, born at Thelveton, near her home. They lived in Woodbridge. Edward was a chemist so a rare move for a Smith out of the milling/farming community. They appear here with their son Edward wearing a dress, so not yet "breeched", in front of an unusually decorated doorway in a conservatory. Joanna died, aged about 40, in 1895.

The lower picture shows Woodbridge Harbour. We can see a Thames sailing barge and the tide mill on a site used since 1170. The present building is from 1793 and now a museum.

Seckford Almhouses, Woodbridge.

This grand building dates from 1834 and still functions as a much-extended residential complex for the elderly. In 1587 Queen Elizabeth I granted Thomas Seckford permission to build almshouses "to relieve need and distress for thirteen local men". He also owned the tide mill.

Stocks at Ufford.

William took a walk to nearby Ufford. Ignoring the fine church with its famous telescopic medieval font cover, his interest was captured by the "Stocks at Ufford". It is by the church gate and a buttress of the church appears here. These stocks can still be seen.

Ipswich Docks

While at Woodbridge William took the train to nearby Ipswich and visited the docks. The lock admitted ships to the inner harbour in which ships are visible. The "Thistle" was about ten years old, built in Glasgow; 165 feet long, it was built of iron. It was wrecked in 1917. The Duke of Hamilton owned Eaton Park near Woodbridge.

Duke of Hamilton Yacht "Thistle"

Ipswich Lock gates

Family Visit 3: Ovington

William's sister Emma was married to Frederick Womack from Fersfield, a few miles from Dickleburgh. He was a farmer, and here we see them at Ovington near Watton. The house can still be seen, well off the road and away from the village. The farm was probably a tenancy and large enough to employ ten men nicely posed here with a wagon. The family eventually had four daughters and a son, so from census information we can date these photographs at around 1889. We also know that the governess was Grace E. Ruffle from Essex and the maids were Emma Tennant from Essex and Millicent Frost from Beeston in Norfolk. William's journey here by train was via changes at Norwich and Thetford and from Watton by pony and trap.

Visit to Newmarket

We do not know who William visited, but they make a good group and it is an impressive house. Another easy journey by train.

"Fairstead House" Newmarket

Family Visits

William photographed a number of local houses belonging to local celebrities.

Lord Waveney, George Leggett Esq., according to William White's History, Gazetteer and Directory of Norfolk, 1883, was a farmer and owner of Pulham Hall. The gazetteer says, "The Hall anciently a seat of a younger branch of the Percy family, was rebuilt by the late J. Crickmore Esq. and is now the property of George Leggett Esq. who occupies it".

Mr. Parker, a farmer, is presumably, the man by the front door.

ODDS AND ENDS

AS he got towards the end of his first album William seems to have found himself with some miscellaneous left-over photographs. These are some of those, not as he arranged them. He did his own cropping and squeezed several onto a page. His captions explain themselves. We think they all have something to say.

20 Miles an hour

The train is distant but the locomotive, running tender first, and the six-wheel coaches can be seen clearly. The bridge is again the Harleston bridge.

Fressingfield Horse Show

In the Hay Field

The first album ends with the "elephant photograph". It is taken from the balcony of Mill House in Harleston. The elephants have attracted some interest but you have to look very closely to see a man in charge standing between them. The travelling circus was a feature of Victorian life and visited even quite small towns each year with acts including Indian elephants. It is known that a circus used to visit Harleston.

Local folklore is that one year a youth teased an elephant in the street and the next year the elephant sought out the same youth and chased him. Elephants never forget!

The house on the left is Candlers named after the doctor who lived there. It still looks much the same. The inn in the centre is the Duke William. Robert Murray was licensee until 1903. It survived as an inn into the 21st century. Since closure it has lost its inn sign. The shop to the right was soon to be replaced. Its owner is not one of our Smiths. William did not caption this photograph: it is actually on one of his left-overs pages inside the back cover. The bottom photograph, taken a decade later, shows the corner of the new and surviving building.

The photograph captioned "Gypsy Cart" explains itself.

Gypsy Cart

We come to the second album and enter the 1890s. William included a greater proportion of family photographs, many of which we have had to omit. However, in this first photograph, his father appears in the Dickleburgh Mill House garden. It is winter and the church is dimly visible.

Shotford Bridge

Another winter scene, a view from the other direction of an earlier photograph. Much the same today but many more trees.

ODDS AND ENDS

Above: *Starston Bridge*

This is the Beck, busy today with cars.

Below: *Mr. Palmer. Starston*

This is Beck Hall. It is also just off the top picture to the left. The meadows near the Beck were farmed by Mr. Palmer.

Two photographs in the Mill House yard at Harleston. One dog moved during the long exposure. The yard buildings were converted into the pottery in about 1970, but the doors and gates are recognisable today.

Carved by Godbold, Harleston

By chance we discovered that Robert Godbold, woodcarvers, had premises next door to the Mill House. Robert was born in 1837 at Bungay where his family name is still well known. His son, also Robert, was his apprentice in 1871, so twenty years later these two pieces may be by either or both. We do not know where these pieces were commissioned for, nor whether they are still in existence.

There are several well known examples of this type of font cover from medieval times in Suffolk churches. They were lifted by a rope from their apex and that at Ufford is "telescopic". In the nineteenth century the Gothic revival and the building of many new churches led to many examples such as this one.

NORWICH, NEEDHAM AND FORNCETT

Norwich was 35 minutes by train from William's home, and the Smith's mill premises were very near the station. The Cattle Market no longer exists; in fact, most "cattle" here are sheep! Lots of detail visible with a magnifying glass.

Norwich Cathedral, West Front.

St. Ethelbert's Gate Norwich

Needham Watermill

Needham is a village near Harleston on the road to Diss. William ignored its very attractive church and took only these two of the Watermill on the River Waveney. This is about a mile upstream from Weybread Mill. The buildings remain but little of these views is visible today.

Forncett

These photographs give little away about what is happening. Forncett is a few miles from Dickleburgh; it had a station but perhaps the pony and trap tell us how William got there with his brother Sam and his brother in law Henry Hudson, both millers. They are in their Sunday best. There was, at Forncett, a Mr. Gardiner who had four daughters and was a farmer. It may have been a business meeting, a visit to friends or even two bachelors… ?

Mr. Gardiner's Forncett

CHURCHES

A number of churches appear in the albums. Here are four arranged by William.

Weybread. Suffolk.

The village is about a mile uphill from the Watermill.

Starston. Norfolk.

The Beck and bridge from previous shots are at the bottom of the hill on the right.

Cratfield. Suffolk.

A few miles to south-east of Harleston and, by report, one of Suffolk's most interesting churches.

Flixton. Suffolk.

East of Harleston and near the Waveney, this is a 19th century church designed by the architect Anthony Salvin. The tower appears to be modelled on the famous Saxon one at Sompting in Sussex and the rest is a mixture of Norman and Gothic. The vicar was a Reverend Smith, possibly a relative, which would explain why four photographs were taken here.

LOWESTOFT AND LINGWOOD

WILLIAM'S father, also William, had retired and moved to Lowestoft by 1891, with his unmarried daughter, Eliza. He died in 1897. William senior lived on Marine Parade in the quite large, three storey terraced houses famously advertised when new as "superior second-class" dwellings. William Rayson probably visited frequently and we have nearly fifty photographs, mostly taken near to his father's home. These will form a second book to be published at a later date. There seem to have been family gatherings and this photograph was perhaps a birthday picture. We think it shows William senior's five daughters, three of his sons and some in-laws. William Rayson is second from the left. The photograph album in the picture is not one of ours though much like them in appearance. This is a good example of William Rayson's ability to get good portraits as each person is focussing on the camera and revealing personality. He did not, of course, click the shutter here.

A fine portrait of William senior and a family gathering on another occasion. Much architectural detail here at the rear of the "superior second-class" house and evidence of laundering and lawn mowing too.

The Rix Family at Lingwood

William's sister, Mary, and Spencer Rix from the earlier photograph at South Walsham with their completed family. By this time - the mid-1890s – Spencer Rix was a well-to-do merchant dealing, among other things, in whisky marketed under his own name. He rented not only Lingwood Manor as their home but also a warehouse near the station from which he operated a mail order business with next day delivery by train. He was eventually bankrupt. After his death, his wife went to live with Jen's grandparents in Lowestoft because, as Jen's mother said, "She had nowhere else to go." It is because of that move that the photographs came eventually to be found in her granddaughter's house.

WILLIAM AS PHOTOGRAPHER

WILLIAM and Winifred seem to have done things together, not least when she pressed the shutter for mutual snapshots. Here we have a beautiful tricycle of which many varieties were made at the time. We assume this might be William's own mode of transport. There is a bell and a front brake, hard tyres but probably no gears. The brake-block seems to be the T-shaped item above the front wheel. The photographs are taken near the front gate of the Mill House in Harleston. One baby chick is visible.

The bottom right picture is technically clever with the slow shutter speeds available on a Victorian camera. William is about 55 years old here.

Stanton's Gala 1892

In the *Diss Express* of the 9th September 1892 Stanton's Gala was announced. It was described as, "An unparalleled Fete on grounds a-joining Park Fields, Diss on Thursday Sept. 15th 1892. Most attractive fete now held in the Eastern Counties." There would be military stage bands and a procession and a free tea at 1 o'clock.

This photograph is of people in Harleston coming home off the train after going to the Gala.

Hospital Sunday

Hospital Saturdays and Sundays were established from about 1860 to appeal for funding for local hospitals.

This photograph also seems to be of people coming home off the train with a band. There is another photograph with a different band.

From the top of the chimney

Looking East

Looking South

The chimney is that of the mill and stood immediately behind the viewpoint used for the two photographs on the previous page. It would not have been a large chimney. A contemporary account says that it was climbed inside using four-inch nails. We can imagine William at the top with his camera supported on the rim of the chimney. The upper view looks over the town. The new church and the clock tower can just be seen. This photograph reminds us of the use of coal fires and the smoky atmosphere of that time. The lower view shows the roof and yard of the Duke William.

The Railway

The original station had a single platform and cramped goods yard, unusual because there were three sidings accessible only via a wagon turntable. This could not be used by a locomotive so shunting would have been done by a horse, accounting for the central position of the horses in two photographs. These are actually "before and after" views. The alterations, that took place in 1884, included a second platform and an enlarged goods yard. There are many details here. Photographs one and two seem to show work in progress that has been temporarily halted and posed for the photographer. The third photograph shows the new platform and footbridge, with mostly station staff.

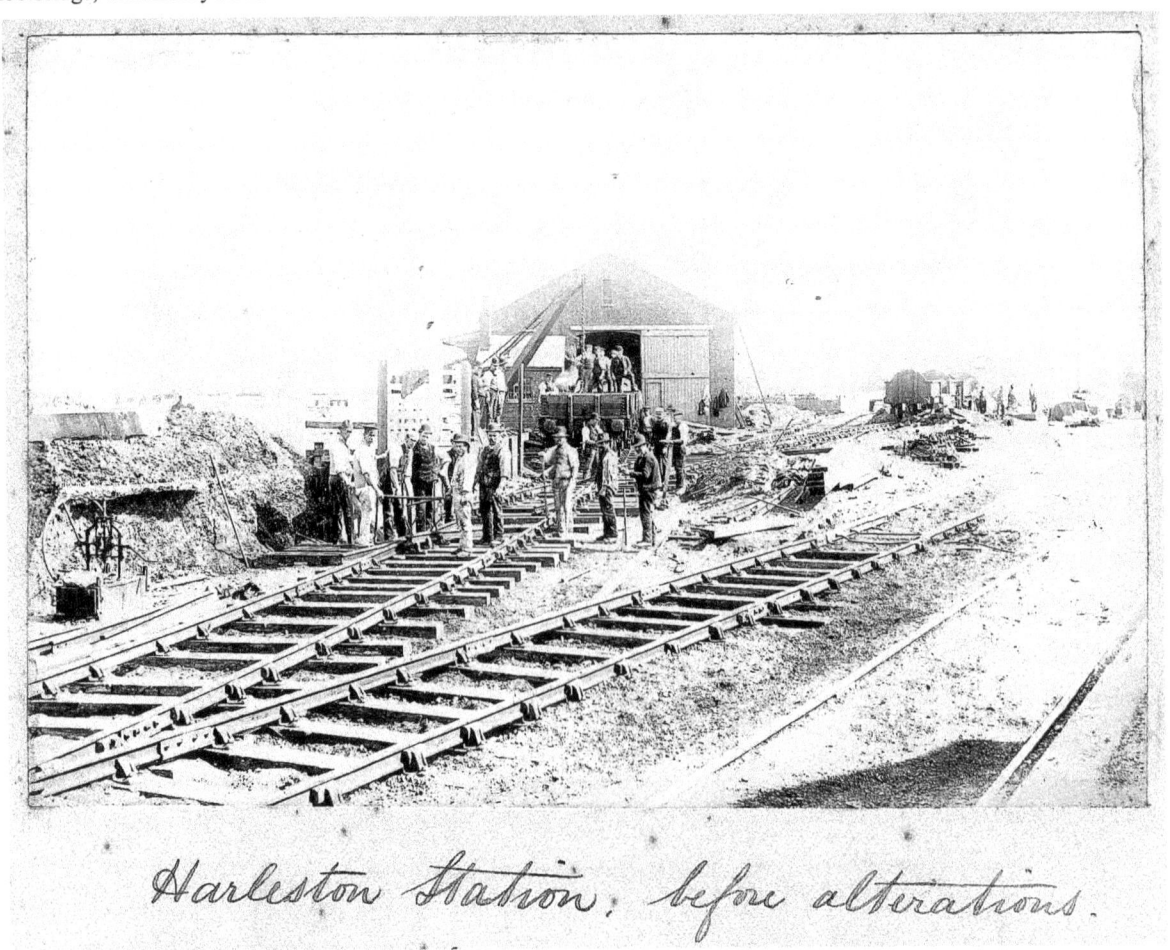

Harleston Station, before alterations.

This photograph shows the Corn Mill (right), which had its own siding between it and the cottages. On either side were malthouses also served by private sidings. The notice on the mill reads: "W. Edwards. Corn, Cake, Manure Merchant & C." The chimney perhaps gives some idea of the size of the Hudson Mill just down the road. These mills were, in fact, small examples of Victorian industrial architecture. The mills and maltings are gone, whilst Hudson's Mill survives, minus the chimney. The cottages still exist.

Harleston Station with alterations

We see the new platform with its buildings and footbridge. The road bridge is visible in the distance. There is a signal box on the main platform. This box does not appear on the other photograph so must also have been new. Here the level crossing gates are open for trains or, perhaps, for the photographer. The horse drawn wagon, labelled GREAT (EASTERN) RAILWAY COMPANY 805, gives us some clues as to the variety of goods brought in by rail.

Floods Homersfield. Oct. 1892

Floods were, and still are, a feature of the Waveney Valley, but this is also a railway photograph. We can see Homersfield Station on the left in very good detail. The Beck stream joined the Waveney to the left, passing under the railway.

Train Trip to Bedford

Winifred Colman went to school in Bedford and seems to have remained friends with someone there after leaving school. In 1891 Winifred was a boarder at 24 London Road in the St. Paul's district of Bedford. Bedford was, at the time, the home of innovative education for girls. Two schools founded by the Sir William Hartley Legacy in 1882 were the Dame Alice Harper School, later the Bedford Girls' Modern School, and Bedford High School for Girls, both on the same site. Here we see a photograph taken on a visit there, with William and Maria to the right of a group of otherwise unknown people. In a companion photograph Winifred replaces William. The journey was via Norwich and Cambridge and probably possible on a day trip. We include one of several local sights.

Near Woburn Sands, Bedfordshire

Bunyans Monument, Bedford

Train Trip to Sheringham

The railway runs from Norwich so this would be an easy day trip. William walked to nearby Beeston and took eight photographs—quite a weight of glass plates to carry. Most interesting was fishermen on the beach. The men often posed for photographs and this appears to be the case here. The writing on the metalwork curiously includes the words FREMANTLE WESTERN AUSTRALIA, and the figures 14/93 and No.127. The rail was maybe destined for export to service the Western Australian gold rush (1885-1893), but here are probably being used as "ways" or "skids" for easy passage of the boats to and from the water.

BILLINGFORD

BILLINGFORD is five miles west of Harleston. The church and Hall stand isolated from other houses and look today much as they do in William's photographs. The only wedding photograph in the albums is this one of his brother-in-law Ernest Hudson and Florence Flowerdew, whose father was the occupant of the Hall and a farmer. The wedding took place in September 1894. We can see the group is posed in front of the Hall with floral decorations for the event around the porch. The groom is in army uniform: he was a surgeon or army doctor. His brother Henry is sixth from the left and Sam Smith and William's wife on the right. Winifred's face is half hidden behind the bride. Both were born in 1874 so possibly Winifred was a bridesmaid. Ernest and Florence had one child of whom there will be more to tell.

A pleasant rural scene taken from near the church, showing Billingford Hall and farm.

PICNICS AND CELEBRATIONS

WILLIAM dated several photographs near the end of his albums. Here we have a variety of picnics and an insight into late Victorian catering customs. Family members appear in each one, but also many unidentified people.

PicNic. Heath House Gravel Pit Aug. 1893 (N.B. William's spelling)

This is just over Shotford Bridge by the Waveney. Whilst neighbouring pits are now flooded, this one remains dry.

Sept. 1893

As in the top picture there is a group of older ladies provided with seats.

July 1894

A picnic by the River Waveney. Did they all sail there in the two boats? The small dog on Maria Smith's knee appears in later photographs.

August 1896

Many girls apparently in uniform are to be seen, some rather rakish-looking men and a formidable lady with a teapot.

Carnival on the river Waveney Feb. 13th–1895

This is a photograph of the Ice Carnival of 1885 that took place between Needham and Weybread Mill when the river froze over. A report in the Norwich News of 1895 describes the event:

> A large number of skaters were attired in fancy dress. The band of the E.D.R.A. Volunteers were in attendance, and discoursed some excellent selections of music under the leadership of Bandmaster E. Burgess. In the evening the river was brilliantly illuminated. This, and various colours worn by the skaters made a charming scene. Shortly after ten a start was made for home, the band marching around the town to the Market Place where the company dispersed. The whole affair was arranged by Mr. J. Spink of Needham, who spared no pains to make the affair a success. Collections were made on behalf of the deserving poor of the parishes of Needham and Harleston. It was estimated that there were about 2000 people present.

Picnics and Celebrations

Jubilee. Harleston 1897

Taken from the upstairs window in the Magpie Inn this shows a band celebrating Queen Victoria's 60 years as Queen.

William's only interior shot is taken in a room that can still be identified in the oldest part of the Mill House. We recognise the dog and a painting of Redenhall Church along with various other items, typical of a Victorian sitting room. These pictures are mounted on the same page.

AN INTIMATE CONCLUSION

THE penultimate page in William's second album has two photographs taken in the Mill House yard. The top photograph is of Frank and Albert Rix. The lower one is a Hudson family group with Winifred.

September 1899

AN INTIMATE CONCLUSION   79

This is William's last picture in his albums. It is a touching family group—probably so for William and Maria when it was taken, but more so in later years. The picture shows the couple married at Billingford, Ernest and Florence Hudson, and their daughter Eleanor, born in India in 1895. The 1901 census shows her, aged 5, living with William, Maria, Winifred and Henry, Maria's brother, at Mill House, Harleston. It seems likely that Ernest, an army surgeon, had been posted to India, returned home on furlough, leaving Eleanor in England in the care of his sister Maria, for her education. So, William took this photograph as a record of a family soon to be parted. A double sadness is that Ernest died, in 1916, in India so William and Maria may never have seen them together again.

September 1899

EPILOGUE

THERE is a so far unanswered question. Why do we know of no more photographs? Did William give up photography at this point or are there more photographs to be found?

We have little information about William's life in Harleston in the years until his death in 1932 aged 91. Maria predeceased him in 1924. He is described in the censuses as "of private means" but we do not know where his money came from. When Maria's brother Henry sold the Mill House in 1905 to marry the widow of the publican of the Magpie Inn, in Harleston, the Smiths lived with them. Eventually the Smiths ended up in a property called "Elmhurst" in Redenhall Road. We know this was a tenancy. William never owned his own house. In those years in Harleston William became a magistrate or J.P. He was the secretary of the Harleston Technical Education Committee. He was a Freemason. His money was left to Winifred.

There is, however, a rather nice tailpiece. There are two letters William wrote to his nephew Hugh Rix in what was then Basutoland. They date from 1928 and 1929. The first is a thankyou to Hugh for some South African postage stamps. So, William was a stamp collector. The second has family news. He writes that he has included "some old photographs of our ancestors". He talks about his health; it is good except for his declining eyesight. Then he writes "I went to Dickleburgh the other day on my bicycle and enjoyed the ride. We Smiths were in Dickleburgh for over 150 years." This is a man of 88 years of age! Dickleburgh is about five miles from Harleston. It ties in nicely with our picture of William on his tricycle aged about 50. Does it suggest also that his main means of local transport had always been his bicycle and on foot, with most of the places he photographed further afield reachable by train?

We include a final photograph of William. It is undated but comes from his final years. William is buried in Dickleburgh churchyard with some of his ancestors, directly across the street from his birthplace.

We have been fascinated by our close examination of William's albums. The information they contain is tantalising – most places are named, but no people. We still do not know who everyone is. We have visited most of the places depicted and done much research in censuses and other records. We have tried to give accurate information and to acknowledge gaps in our knowledge. We hope our selection of 125 photographs will prove interesting to readers. Those photographs taken in Lowestoft will appear in a second book.

Please would anyone who has any further information contact us via our email address: jmdjb@outlook.com. We will be very grateful.

CHARACTER LIST

THIS list is to aid the understanding of the photographs. It will be of interest to some who know of the families but a detailed family history is not intended.

The Smith Family from Dickleburgh

William Smith 1   1748–1812

William Smith 2   1786–1862

William Smith 3   1812–1897: 1881 census: a widower; 1891 census: lived in Lowestoft.

William Smith's children, spouses and their children:

Anna Rayson Smith b. 1838, unmarried, lived with Samuel.

Harriet Smith   1840–1856

William Rayson Smith 1841–1932 m. Maria Hudson in 1866, adopted daughter, Winifred Annie Colman. (N.B. Also spelt Winnifred in some early records.)

Walter Smith   1844–1853

Eliza Smith   b. 1845, unmarried, lived with her father in Dickleburgh and Lowestoft.

Mary Smith   b. 1846 m. Henry Spencer Rix (farmer and merchant). Lived South Walsham and Lingwood. Eight children including twins born in 1886.

Alfred Smith   b. 1847

Emma Smith   b. 1848 m. Edward Eaton (chemist). Lived in Woodbridge. One son, Edward b. 1886

Samuel Smith   b. 1850

Joanna Smith   b. 1854 m. Frederick Womack (farmer). Lived in Ovington. Five children.

Horace Smith   b. 1857 m. Mary Marsters Patrick. One son, Ivan, b. 1886 in Montreal, Canada. Lived in Lowestoft in 1891.

The Hudson Family from Harleston

Henry Lombard Hudson 1816–1885 m. Caroline 1812–1894

Henry Lombard and Caroline Hudson's children, spouses and their children:

Maria Hudson   b. 1843 m. William Rayson Smith. Winifred Annie Colman, "adopted daughter".

Thompson Hudson b. 1844

Elizabeth Hudson b. 1845

Henry Hudson   b. 1848 unmarried.

Louisa Hudson   b. 1852

Ernest Hudson   b. 1859 m. Florence Flowerdew, Sept. 1894. One daughter, Eleanor, b.1895 in India.

BIBLIOGRAPHY AND ACKNOWLEDGEMENTS

Anderson R. & Kenworthy G., *Tivetshall to Beccles: The Waveney Line* (Middleton Press, 2004)

Cautley, H. M., *Suffolk Churches and their Treasures* (Boydell Press, 1954)

Mayes T. & Neville D., *Whatever Happened to the Half Moon?* (Harleston Heritage Group, 2006)

Peart S., *The Book of Lingwood* (Halsgrove, 2013)

White, R., *Discovering Old Cameras* 1839–1939 (Shire Publishing, 1995)

Other Reference Material

U.K. and Canada Censuses

O.S. Maps

Norfolk Mills website

Norfolk Heritage Explorer website

Kelly's Directories

William White's History, Gazeteer and Directory of Norfolk 1888

Acknowledgements and thanks to:

Representatives of Harleston Museum.

Representatives of the Dickleburgh Village Society.

Matt Rix for his willingness to share family history knowledge, the photograph of W. R. Smith in his later years, and the letters of W.R. Smith to Hugh Rix, his Great Grandfather.

Carol Jones for proof reading our text.

Gareth H. H. Davies for the maps.

INDEX

Allen Line, 29

Bedford
    Bunyan's Monument, 70
    Woburn Sands, 70
    Schools, 70

Billingford, 72-73, 79

Brandreth
    Henry, The Rev., 16, 23
    Louisa, 16

Bicycles, 65, 70, 80

Bure, River, 43

Burston, 11

cameras, 10, 11, 30, 37, 62, 65, 68

Canada
    Belleville, 7, 24, 30
        Post Office, 24
        suspension bridge, 28
    Bohemian, 29
    Cornwall Town, 29
    Parisian, 29
    Prescott, 29
    timber, 26-27

Churches, 60

Colman, Winifred Annie, 9, 19, 30, 31, 36, 65, 70, 72, 78, 79, 80, 81

Cornwall Line, 29

Cratfield, 61

Dickleburgh, 11
    Church, 9, 14, 21
    Churchyard, 9, 20
    Crown Inn, 13
    Corn Mill, 11, 15
    Hall, 18
    Jubilee, 1887, 7, 22-23
    Lee Cottage, 11, 16-17
    Mill House, 9, 15, 19, 53
    Millhouse Garden, 17, 53
    Moor, 30
    Corner House, 13
    Mill Yard, 15
    Rectory, 21

Eaton
    Joanna, 44
    Edward, 44

elephants, 7, 52

Flixton, 61

Flowerdew, Florence, 72

Forncett, 59

Fressingfield Horse Show, 50

Gardiner, Mr., 59

Godbold, 55

graves, 14, 20

gypsy cart, 51

Harleston
    Candlers, 51
    Duke William, The, 51, 67
    Jubilee
        1887, 7, 38
        1897, 77
    Magpie Inn, 9, 77, 80
    Mill House, 9, 30, 31, 41, 51, 54, 55, 65, 77, 78, 79, 80
    Railway Bridge, 37
    Thoroughfare, 40
    Windmill, 34
    Station, 7, 36, 37, 68, 69

Heath House Gravel Pit, 74

Homersfield, floods, 69

Hospital Saturdays and Sundays, 7, 66

Hudson, 78
    Eleanor, 79
    Ernest. 79
    Florence, 79
    Henry Lombard, 9, 30, 34, 59
    Maria, 9

Hudson Mill, 68

Ice Carnival, 76

Ipswich Docks, 46
    Thistle, 46

Leggett, Mr., 49

Lingwood, 64

Lowestoft, 7, 36, 40, 63, 64, 80

Needham, 56, 76
    Watermill, 58

Newmarket, 36, 48
    Fairstead House, 48

Norwich
    Cattle Market, 56
    Castle Hill, 56
    Cathedral, 57

Ovington, 47

Palmer, Mr., 53
Parker, Mr., 49
photography, 9. 24, 80
picnics, 74-75
Pulham Hall, 49

Queen Victoria, 7, 23, 77

railway, 36-37, 68-69, 70-71
Redenhall, 9, 40, 77
Rix
    Albert, 78
    Frank, 78
    Hugh, 80
    Mary, 7, 42, 64
    Spencer, 42, 64

Seckford Almhouses, 45

Sheringham, 36, 71
Shotford Bridge, 32, 52, 74
Smith
    Anne, 9
    Eliza, 62
    Emma, 47
    Joanna, 44
    Mary, 9
    Samuel, 9
    Sarah, 9
    William 1, 9
    William 2, 20
    William 3 (father of William Rayson), 9, 62-63
    William Rayson 7, 9-11, 20, 24, 30, 32, 34, 36, 40, 42, 46-50, 51-52, 58-59, 60, 62, 65, 67, 70-71, 74, 79, 80
South Walsham, 42-43, 64
Stanton Gala, 66
Starston
    Beck Hall, 53
    Jubilee Sports, 38

Tivetshall, 20, 36
Trains (see railway)

Ufford (stocks), 45

Waveney, River, 7, 32, 34, 58, 61, 74, 75, 76
Weybread, 34, 60
Water Mill, 34, 76
Womack
    Emma (see Smith)
    Frederick, 47
Woodbridge, 46
    Harbour, 44

www.ingramcontent.com/pod-product-compliance
Lightning Source LLC
Chambersburg PA
CBHW080010050426
42446CB00036B/3331